I0801140

MANNERS MATTER TO MAEVIS

Maevis HAS GOOD ATTENDANCE

Written by
Vicky Bureau
M.S., School Counseling

Illustrated by
Flavia Zuncheddu

A Starfish Book
SEAHORSE
PUBLISHING

Teaching Tips for Caregivers:

As a caregiver, you can help your child succeed in school by giving them a strong foundation in language and literacy skills and a desire to learn to read.

This book helps children grow by letting them practice reading skills.

Reading for pleasure and interest will help your child to develop reading skills and will give your child the opportunity to practice these skills in meaningful ways.

- Encourage your child to read on her own at home
- Encourage your child to practice reading aloud
- Encourage activities that require reading
- Establish a reading time
- Talk with your child
- Give your child writing materials

Teaching Tips for Teachers:

Research shows that one of the best ways for students to learn a new topic is to read about it.

Before Reading

- Read the "Words to Know" and discuss the meaning of each word.
- Read the back cover to see what the book is about.

During Reading

- When a student gets to a word that is unknown, ask them to look at the rest of the sentence to find clues to help with the meaning of the unknown word.
- Ask the student to write down any pages of the book that were confusing to them.

After Reading

- Discuss the main idea of the book.
- Ask students to give one detail that they learned in the book by showing a text dependent answer from the book.

TABLE OF CONTENTS

Meet Maevis 4
Being on Time 10
Being Late 12
Words to Know 22
Index 23
Comprehension Questions 23
About the Author 24

Meet Maevis

This is Maevis.

School **manners** matter to Maevis.

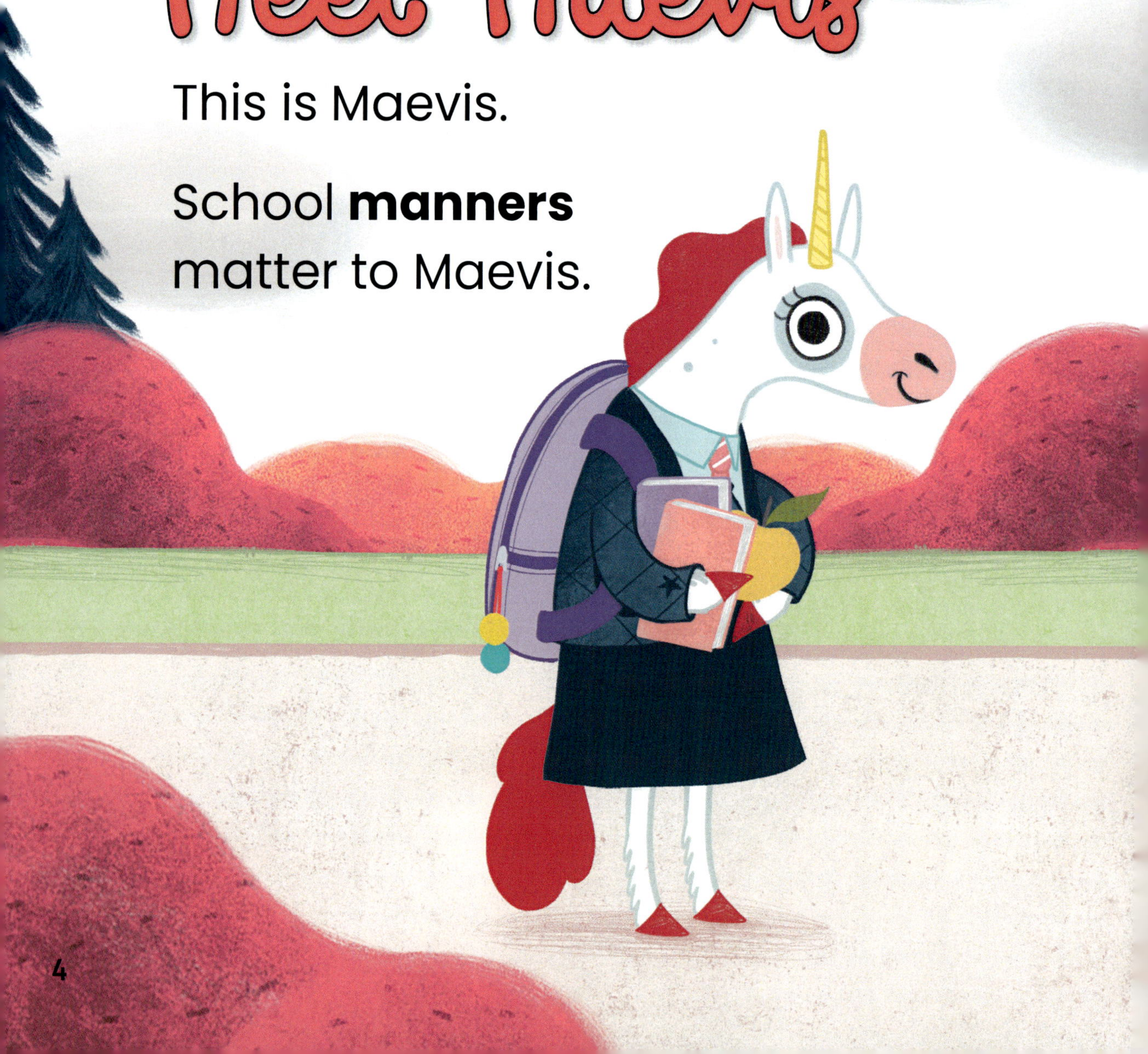

School manners are the rules and expectations for learning.

One important school manner is **attendance**.

Attendance means that Maevis is present at school.

Being present means that Maevis is in her seat and ready to learn.

Maevis is not at home or on vacation.

Being on Time

It's also important to be on time.

On time means that Maevis is at school when the morning bell rings.

Being Late

If Maevis is not on time, she is late.

Late means that Maevis has arrived at school after the first bell has rung.

Maevis might need a **tardy** pass.

Sometimes, something **unexpected** can come up.

Then, Maevis cannot come to school.

Or she cannot help being late.

Maevis might be sick.

Or her mom might run into **traffic**.

Being present and on time is important to Maevis because it helps her learn!

Manners matter to Maevis.

And that’s why Maevis has good attendance!

A+
PERFECT
ATTENDANCE

WORDS TO KNOW

attendance (uh-TEN-duhns): the act of being present at a place or an event

manners (MAN-urs): the rules and expectations for learning; good behaviors

tardy (TAHR-dee): late or delayed

traffic (TRAF-ik): the slow movement of vehicles or persons in an area or along a street

unexpected (uhn-ik-SPEK-tid): not expected or foreseen; surprising

INDEX

important 6, 10, 18
late 12, 13, 15
on time 10, 18
present 7, 8, 18
rules 5
school 4, 5, 6, 7, 10, 13, 14

COMPREHENSION QUESTIONS

1. What does it mean to be on time?
2. What does it mean to be late?
3. Why is it important for Maevis to be on time to school?
4. What happens if Maevis arrives to school after the first bell rings?

ABOUT THE AUTHOR

Vicky Bureau was born in Longueuil, Quebec, and was raised in South Florida. As a teacher, she developed a passion for the social and emotional growth of her students and later transitioned into the area of child and adolescent psychology after earning her master's degree in school counseling.
In addition to working with children, Vicky loves to be surrounded by animals and nature. She lives in Fort Lauderdale with her family: Billy, Khloe, M.J., and Max; her three cats, Alley, Baguette, and Salem; and her dog, Boomer.

Written by: Vicky Bureau
Illustrated by: Flavia Zuncheddu
Design by: Under the Oaks Media
Editor: Kim Thompson

Library of Congress PCN Data
Maevis Has Good Attendance / Vicky Bureau
Manners Matter to Maevis
ISBN 978-1-63897-460-4(hard cover)
ISBN 978-1-63897-575-5(paperback)
ISBN 978-1-63897-690-5(EPUB)
ISBN 978-1-63897-805-3(eBook)
Library of Congress Control Number: 2022932686

Printed in Canada/042024/CPC20240426

Seahorse Publishing Company
www.seahorsepub.com

Copyright © 2023 **SEAHORSE PUBLISHING COMPANY**
All rights reserved. No part of this publication may be reproduced, stored in a retrieval system or be transmitted in any form or by any means, electronic, mechanical, photocopying, recording, or otherwise, without the prior written permission of Seahorse Publishing Company.

Published in the United States
Seahorse Publishing
PO Box 771325
Coral Springs, FL 33077

SEAHORSE PUBLISHING